Discovering and Exploring the Americas

BY
CINDY BARDEN

COPYRIGHT © 2001 Mark Twain Media, Inc.

ISBN 1-58037-174–4

Printing No. CD-1395

Mark Twain Media, Inc., Publishers
Distributed by Carson-Dellosa Publishing Company, Inc.

Table of Contents

1	About the American History Series	32	Was Cortés a Hero?
2	Time Line for *Discovering and Exploring the Americas*	33	Meet Francisco Pizarro
		34	Pizarro Uses Treachery to Defeat the Incas
3	Who Came First?	35	More Treachery
4	Sailing to the Americas	36	Meet Francisco Vasquez de Coronado
5	Meet Leif the Lucky	37	In Search of the Seven Cities of Cíbola
6	Welcome to Vinland	38	What Did Coronado Really Discover?
7	The Lands of the Vikings	39	Meet Hernando de Soto
8	Meet Christopher Columbus	40	De Soto as Governor of Florida
9	The Four Voyages of Columbus	41	Let's Review
10	Fact or Fiction?	42	Interview an Explorer
10	How Big Were Columbus's Ships?	43	Meet Jacques Cartier
11	Trade With the Far East	44	Cartier's Second Voyage
12	Meet Vasco Núñez de Balboa	45	Cartier's Third and Final Voyage
13	Sighting the Pacific Ocean	46	Important Events During Cartier's Lifetime
14	A New Governor Takes Command		
15	Preparing for a Sea Voyage	47	Meet Samuel de Champlain
16	Meet Amerigo Vespucci	48	Father of New France
17	How Vespucci Became Famous	49	Discovering a New World
18	Meet John Cabot	50	Meet Henry Hudson
19	A Charter From the King	51	Hudson's Fate Unknown
20	Searching for Wealth	52	Meet René Robert Cavelier, Sieur de La Salle
21	Meet Sebastian Cabot		
22	The Search Continues	53	A Disastrous Adventure
23	Magellan Circumnavigates the Earth	54	Let's Review
24	Let's Review	55	Which Came First?
25	Meet Juan Ponce de León	56	Where Were They From?
26	A Frustrating Search	57	Setting Up a New Colony
27	The Fountain of Youth	58	Searching for the Explorers
28	In the News	59	Setting Up a Space Colony
29	Meet Hernan Cortés	60	Learn About Other Explorers
30	Cortés Meets Montezuma	61	Answer Key
31	Conquest of the Aztecs		

About the American History Series

Welcome to *Discovering and Exploring the Americas*, one of 12 books in the Mark Twain Media, Inc., American History series for students in grades four to seven.

The activity books in this series are designed as stand-alone material for classrooms and home-schoolers or as supplemental material to enhance your history curriculum. Students can be encouraged to use the books as independent study units to improve their understanding of historical events and people.

Each book provides challenging activities that enable students to explore history, geography, and social studies topics. The activities provide research opportunities and promote critical reading, thinking, and writing skills. As students follow the journeys of famous explorers and learn about the people who influenced history, they will draw conclusions; write opinions; compare and contrast historical events, people, and places; analyze cause and effect; and improve mapping skills. Students will also have the opportunity to apply what they learn to their own lives through reflection and creative writing.

Students can further increase their knowledge and understanding of historical events by using reference sources at the library and on the Internet. Students may need assistance to learn how to use search engines and discover appropriate websites.

Titles of books for additional reading appropriate to the subject matter at this grade level are included in each book.

Although many of the questions are open-ended, an answer key is included at the back of the book for questions with specific answers.

Share a journey through history with your students as you explore the books in the Mark Twain Media, Inc., American History series:

Discovering and Exploring the Americas
Life in the Colonies
The American Revolution
The Lewis and Clark Expedition
The Westward Movement
The Gold Rush
The Oregon and Sante Fe Trails
Slavery
The Civil War
Lincoln
Reconstruction
Industrialization

Time Line for *Discovering and Exploring the Americas*

30,000 B.C. - 4,000 B.C.	Migrations across the Bering Strait to Alaska
about 985 A.D.	Erik the Red discovered Greenland
about 1000	Leif Erikson arrived in North America
1492 - 1502	Columbus made four voyages to the New World
1493	Ponce de León arrived in Santo Domingo
1496	John Cabot's first unsuccessful voyage
1497	John Cabot landed in Newfoundland
1497 - 1499	Vasco da Gama discovered a sea route around Africa
1498	John Cabot, four ships, and crew lost at sea
1499 - 1512	Amerigo Vespucci explored coast of South America
1501	Vasco Balboa arrived in South America
1508	Sebastian Cabot explored Hudson Bay
1509	Ponce de León appointed Governor of Puerto Rico
1513	Vasco de Balboa first saw the Pacific Ocean
1513	Ponce de León searched for the fountain of youth
1519	Hernan Cortés founded Veracruz
1520	Ferdinand Magellan sailed from Spain, around South America, to India
1521	Hernan Cortés conquered the Aztec Empire in Mexico
1524	Hernan Cortés led an expedition to Honduras
1526	Sebastian Cabot set off on a four-year voyage
1530	Francisco Pizarro conquered the Incas of Peru
1534 - 1541	Jacques Cartier made three voyages to Newfoundland
1536	Hernan Cortés discovered Baja California
1537	Hernando de Soto appointed Governor of Florida
1538	Francisco de Coronado appointed Governor of New Galicia
1539 - 1542	Hernando de Soto explored southeastern United States
1540 - 1541	Francisco de Coronado searched for the Seven Cities of Cíbola
1541	Hernando de Soto first saw the Mississippi River
1607 - 1608	Henry Hudson searched for a shortcut to India for the Muscovy Company
1608	Samuel de Champlain helped found Quebec
1610	Henry Hudson explored the Hudson River for the Dutch East India Company, giving the Netherlands claim to land around New York
1610	Henry Hudson set adrift in Hudson Bay by mutineers
1633	Samuel de Champlain became Governor of New France
1682	Robert La Salle explored the Mississippi River to the Gulf of Mexico
1684	Robert La Salle sent to establish a French colony at the mouth of the Mississippi River

Name: _____ Date: _____

Who Came First?

The first people to discover the New World weren't famous Europeans. They weren't sailors or explorers searching for a new world. Who were they? How did they get to the Americas? From where did they come? Why did they come? When did they arrive?

Although the names of those who first journeyed to North America are not recorded, we do know a little about them and how they traveled. The first people to arrive in the Americas didn't sail here in large ships—they walked—thousands of miles across Siberia to Alaska. During the ice ages, a land bridge connected the two continents.

Small groups of nomads began arriving in North America about 30,000 years ago. As they traveled, migrating groups might settle for a time in a place that offered good hunting or fishing. Some stayed for a year or two or even many, many years before moving on. Eventually, some of the group or their descendents continued the journey, following the migrating herds of animals they hunted.

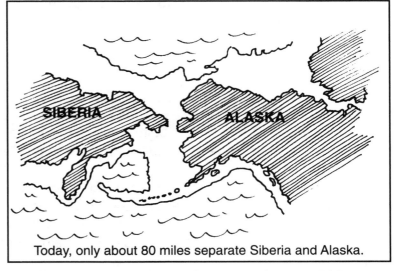

Today, only about 80 miles separate Siberia and Alaska.

Not all groups made the journey at the same time. Many waves of migrants crossed the Siberian land bridge during a period covering more than 25,000 years. The last migration occurred about 4,000 years ago.

Define these words. Use a dictionary if you need help.

1. explorer: _____

_____

2. descendents: _____

_____

3. migrate: _____

_____

4. nomads: _____

_____

By the time Christopher Columbus set sail from Spain in 1492, thousands of groups of people with many different cultures and languages lived in the Americas.

Name: _____ Date: _____

Sailing to the Americas

Although we usually think of Christopher Columbus as being the first European to visit the Americas, evidence suggests that by the time Columbus set sail, the voyages of the first Europeans to the New World had been long forgotten. Norsemen (Vikings from Scandinavia) sailed from Greenland to Newfoundland where they set up a colony about 500 years before Columbus was even born.

Other sources claim that sailors from Ireland landed in North America about 500 A.D.

The Vikings, also called Norsemen, lived in Scandinavia. Some, like Erik the Red, settled in Iceland and later in Greenland.

1. Use reference sources to name the modern countries that make up Scandinavia:

_____

Where they landed and built settlements is uncertain. Viking ruins found in northern Newfoundland, a province of Canada, suggest that at least one settlement was in that area.

Stories of the life and adventures of Erik the Red, Leif the Lucky, and other Viking explorers were handed down orally for about 200 years before being written. The original documents have been lost, and only copies written in the 1300s and 1400s remain. Europeans who read about the adventures and explorations of the Vikings may have believed they were only made-up stories.

In 1964, President Lyndon B. Johnson and Congress officially recognized Leif Erikson as the first European to land in North America by proclaiming October 9 as "Leif Ericson Day."

2. Look carefully at the drawing of this Viking ship. On another sheet of paper, describe what you think it would be like to sail across the ocean in an open ship like this.

Name: _____ Date: _____

Meet Leif the Lucky

Born: sometime after 960 A.D. in Iceland
Died: sometime before 1025, probably in Greenland

Born in Iceland, Leif Erikson was one of three sons of Erik the Red, a man who moved from Norway to Iceland when he was young. About 985 A.D., Leif's father got into trouble and was banished from Iceland for three years. He and a small crew set off to explore the area west of Iceland. It is uncertain whether Leif went with his father, but he probably did because that was the usual custom at the time.

When he returned, Erik reported that he had found a new land with green fields that he named Greenland. He convinced others to move with him and his family to the new land. About 25 ships carrying about 750 people sailed for Greenland, but only 14 ships survived the journey.

Most details about Leif Erikson's life and explorations have been lost. Even his name is not certain. Some sources use the spelling Liev, others, Leif. His last name, meaning "son of Erik", has been spelled Ericson, Eriksson, and Erikson.

Erik the Red became one of Greenland's leaders. He sent Leif on a ship to Norway in 997 A.D. to take presents to King Olaf and to trade furs, walrus and narwhal ivory, woolens, live polar bears, and gyrfalcons for items the colonists needed, like iron, timber, and grains. The king commanded Leif to take the teachings of Christianity back to his people. Evidence of a small church has been found near the area where Erik the Red and his family lived in Greenland, so Leif may have followed the king's command.

As the colony in Greenland grew larger, they had one serious problem — lack of trees for building ships and homes. The few trees that grew there were small and scrubby. Leif had heard stories of other lands beyond Greenland, lands with many large trees. Around the year 1000 A.D., Leif sailed in search of those lands.

1. The names Iceland and Greenland sound very descriptive. Use reference sources to find out more about one of these places. Write a short paragraph on another sheet of paper explaining why you think the name is or is not appropriate.

Name: _____ Date: _____

Welcome to Vinland

The first place Leif and his crew landed was probably Baffin Island. Leif named it Helluland—meaning "Slab Land" or "Flatstone Land." Sailing southwest, they sighted Markland—"Land of Woods," which was probably the coast of Labrador.

Finally they came to a channel that led to a river. They saw large salmon in the water, seabirds in the air, plants, trees, and evidence of animals on land. They called it Vinland—"Land of Meadows"—and spent the winter there. It is uncertain exactly where Leif and his crew landed. It could have been in northern Newfoundland or as far south as Cape Cod, Massachusetts.

On their voyage home the following spring, Leif and his crew rescued sailors who had been shipwrecked on an island off the coast of Greenland. Because of this event and his discovery of Vinland, he was nicknamed Leif the Lucky.

Leif never returned to the land he had discovered. His father died, and Leif took his place as leader of the settlement in Greenland.

Leif's brother Thorvald sailed to the new land, but his voyage wasn't as lucky. While in North America, he was killed by an arrow. Leif's other brother, also named Thorvald, attempted to bring his body back to be buried. Thorvald ran into storms before he could reach Vinland and was forced to return to Greenland where he died a short time later.

Thorfinn Karlsefni made another attempt to settle in Vinland, but hostile natives forced the settlers to abandon their colony and return to Greenland. Even Leif's sister led an expedition of three ships to Vinland, where she was said to have killed the leaders of the other two ships and all their crew.

1. Considering all that happened to him, do you think Leif the Lucky was an appropriate nickname? Why or why not?

_____

_____

_____

_____

_____

Check It Out:
Leif Ericson: Explorer of Vinland by Matthew G. Grant
Leif Erikson The Lucky by Malcolm C. Jensen
Leif Eriksson and the Vikings by Chanan Simon

Name: _____   Date: _____

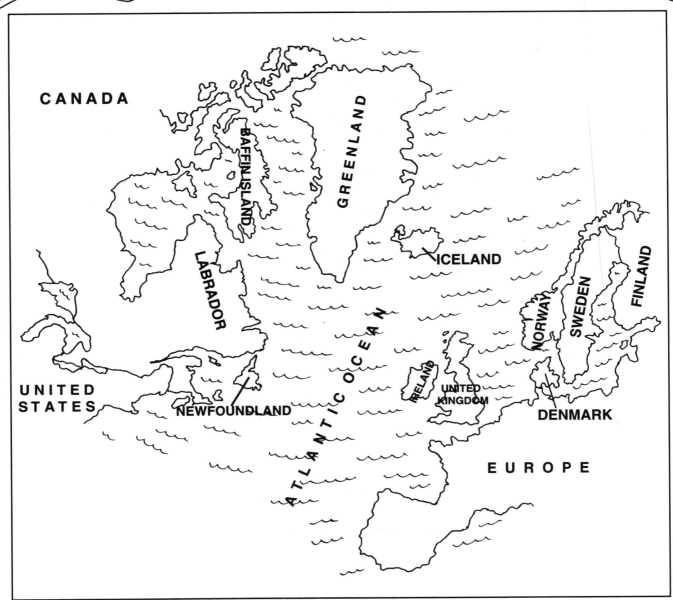

The Lands of the Vikings

1. Use blue to color the land where Erik the Red lived before he was banished for three years.
2. Use green to color the land discovered by Erik the Red.
3. Use brown to color the country where King Olaf ruled.
4. Use red to circle the name of the island Leif the Lucky named Helluland.
5. Use blue to circle the name of the place Leif Erikson called Markland.
6. Use black to outline Newfoundland.

Name: _____   Date: _____

Meet Christopher Columbus

Born: in Genoa, Italy, in 1451
Died: 1506

When he sailed from Spain in 1492, Christopher Columbus was not looking for a new world. Although Columbus and many others believed the earth was round, they simply didn't realize how large it actually was.

Columbus set sail looking for an ocean route to Asia that would be shorter and safer than traveling by land. If indeed the earth was round, it made sense to sail west to reach the lands of the east. Little did anyone realize that a huge land mass, the continents of North and South America, lay between Europe and Asia.

Columbus landed in the Caribbean on an island in the Bahamas, which he named San Salvador. Thinking he had reached the East Indies and had found a new route to Asia, he called the people who lived there Indians. He made three more voyages to the New World. When he died in 1506, he still thought he had found the water route to Asia.

Use reference sources to answer the questions.

The person we know as Christopher Columbus was never known by that name while he was alive. He, himself, used several names to fit the country in which he lived. In Italy, his name was **Cristoforo Colombo**; in Portugal, he became **Cristavao Colom**. To the Spanish, he was **Cristobal Colon**; to the French, he was **Christophe Colombe**. The Latinized version of his name came to be used by English historians. To us, the man will always be **Christopher Columbus**.

1. Who sponsored Christopher Columbus's voyages?

_____

2. In what years did Columbus make his four trips to the New World?

    A. _____   B. _____   C. _____   D. _____

3. List five places in the United States named after Columbus.

_____

_____

_____

Name: _____ Date: _____

The Four Voyages of Columbus

Use the map to answer the questions.

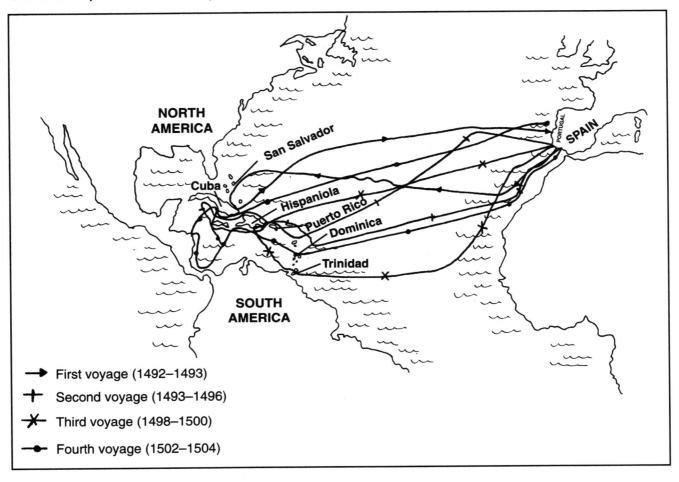

NORTH AMERICA

San Salvador

Cuba

Hispaniola

Puerto Rico

Dominica

Trinidad

SOUTH AMERICA

PORTUGAL SPAIN

→ First voyage (1492–1493)

✛ Second voyage (1493–1496)

✱ Third voyage (1498–1500)

•— Fourth voyage (1502–1504)

1. Trace the first voyage of Columbus in red, the second in green, the third in blue, and the fourth in black.

2. Color Spain blue.

3. The first place Columbus landed was on San Salvador. Circle it in blue.

4. Of the four voyages, which appears to be the longest one?

_____

Check It Out:

If You Were There in 1492 by Barbara Brenner

All Pigs on Deck: Christopher Columbus's Second Marvelous Voyage by Laura Fischetto

Columbus: The Triumphant Failure by Oliver Postgate

Name: _____ Date: _____

Fact or Fiction?

Can you separate fact from fiction? Use reference sources to find the answers. Circle Fact or Fiction for each statement below.

1. Fact or Fiction: In 1474, Columbus was a sailor on a ship attacked and destroyed by pirates. He ended up floating to shore in Portugal.

2. Fact or Fiction: For a time, Columbus worked with his brother Bartholomew in a map shop.

3. Fact or Fiction: Columbus never learned to read or write.

4. Fact or Fiction: Queen Isabella sold her jewels to pay for Columbus's voyage.

5. Fact or Fiction: During his fourth voyage, Columbus was shipwrecked on Jamaica for a year.

6. Fact or Fiction: Columbus started a colony he named Isabela and put his brother Diego in charge.

7. Fact or Fiction: Columbus once made a sailor walk the plank for refusing an order.

8. Fact or Fiction: Two of Columbus's ships, the Niña and Pinta, were given by the town of Palos, Spain, to the king and queen to repay a debt.

How Big Were Columbus's Ships?

1. The three ships Columbus took on his first voyage were not very large. To get an idea of their sizes, use a tape measure and chalk to draw the dimensions of the Niña on the playground, or rope off an area that size in a yard. Invite 24 people inside the ship.

	Length	Width	Crew
Santa Maria	about 82 feet	about 28 feet	40
Pinta	about 74 feet	about 26 feet	26
Niña	about 74 feet	about 24 feet	24

2. What do you think it would have been like for 24 people to spend two months at sea in a boat that size?

_____

_____

_____

10

Name: _____ Date: _____

 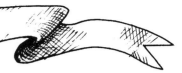

Trade With the Far East

By the mid-14th century, trade had been established between Europe, China, and other countries in Asia. People were willing to pay large amounts of money for the rich silks, exotic spices, and other luxury items from Asia. But the overland route to Asia was long and dangerous. Much of the route was controlled by the Ottoman Turks, who were not friendly to Europeans. A route to Asia around the tip of Africa was not discovered until 1498 by Vasco da Gama.

Use the Internet or other reference sources and the map below to answer the questions. Write your answers on another sheet of paper.

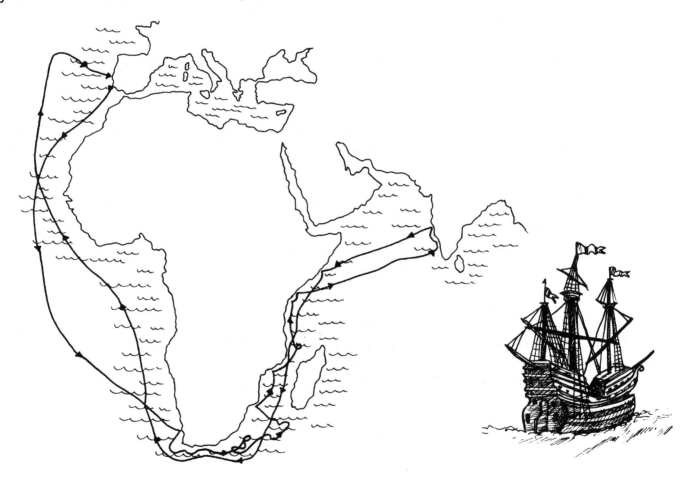

1. What continent did Vasco da Gama sail around to reach India?
2. What did da Gama hope to accomplish by his voyage?
3. What was the trip like?
4. How long was the voyage?
5. What did da Gama's voyage prove?

Check It Out:
Vasco Da Gama and the Portuguese Explorers by Jim Gallagher

Name: _____   Date: _____

Meet Vasco Núñez de Balboa

Born: around 1475 in Jerez de los Caballeros, Spain
Died: 1519

Vasco Núñez de Balboa made his first voyage to the New World in 1501 with Don Rodrigo de Bastidas, a wealthy Spanish nobleman. After exploring the coast of Venezuela and trading with Native Americans, they wanted to return to Spain. Their ships were in bad shape, and they made it only as far as the island of Hispaniola before sinking near shore. Eventually Bastidas returned to Spain, but Balboa stayed in Hispaniola where he became a planter. Seven years later his plantation had failed, and he was deeply in debt.

Considered the first of the Spanish conquistadors (leaders of the Spanish conquest in the New World), Balboa is remembered for being the first European to see the Pacific Ocean.

Anxious to escape his creditors, Balboa convinced a friend to help him hide in a barrel and smuggle him aboard a ship. When discovered, the captain threatened to have Balboa marooned on a deserted island. Luckily, he changed his mind and allowed Balboa to become one of the crew. The captain and his crew built a settlement and named it San Sebastian.

At San Sebastian, men fell ill from lack of food and snake and insect bites. Native Americans attacked frequently with poison-tipped arrows and eventually burned the settlement to the ground.

Balboa suggested the survivors move to the settlement of Darien on the Isthmus of Panama. After a time, Balboa was elected as leader of the town. Food was plentiful in the area and so was gold. Balboa and his men learned to eat new foods including potatoes, corn, and pineapples—crops that did not grow in Europe at that time.

1. The ship Balboa sailed on explored the coast of what country?_____

2. What did Balboa do in Hispaniola? _____

_____

3. How and why did he leave Hispaniola?_____

_____

4. Why had Balboa never eaten potatoes, corn, or pineapple before he came to the New World?

_____

Name: _____ Date: _____

Sighting the Pacific Ocean

Balboa and his men explored the inland areas of Panama and brought Native Americans under Spanish rule. Unlike later conquistadors, Balboa used diplomacy instead of force. He believed it was better to have the native people as friendly neighbors rather than bitter enemies, a lesson many other Spanish leaders never learned.

1. Why do you think this was a wise policy for Balboa to follow?

_____

_____

_____

_____

When the man who had been appointed governor of Darien arrived, Balboa and the other settlers forced him to leave. They believed he would take away everything they had worked to earn.

Although no one else was blamed, Balboa was accused of treason in 1513. Hoping to win back the favor of King Ferdinand, he began searching for the great sea and fabulous cities of gold rumored to be on the other side of the isthmus. Although Balboa found some gold, the fabulous cities he heard about were those of the Incas of Peru, who were later conquered and destroyed by Francisco Pizarro.

2. Use a dictionary to define these words.

   a. diplomacy: _____

   _____

   b. treason: _____

   _____

   c. isthmus: _____

   _____

Balboa led 190 Spanish soldiers and 800 Native Americans across the thick swamps and jungles of Panama. To find the way, he hired guides who took them as far as they could, and then he sent them back with rewards and hired others to continue. On September 29, 1513, they reached the Pacific Ocean. Balboa named it Mar del Sur (South Sea) and claimed it for Spain.

Check It Out:
Vasco Núñez De Balboa by Maureen Ash

Name: _____ Date: _____

A New Governor Takes Command

Balboa sent word of his discovery to the king, plus gifts of gold and pearls, but the king had already sent a new governor, Pedrarias, to Darien.

This is part of a letter from King Ferdinand to Balboa.

... I was rejoiced to read your letters and to learn of the things you discovered ... you will be honored and your services recompensed ... I am pleased with the way you behaved to the chiefs on that march, with kindness and forbearance ... When your letters came, Pedrarias had already left. I am writing to him to look to your affairs with care and to favor you as a person whom I greatly desire to gratify and who has greatly served me, and I am sure that he will do so.

Although Balboa had regained the king's favor, been given the title admiral, and named governor of the South Sea, Panama, and Coiba, the king had left it up to Pedrarias to give Balboa permission for any undertaking. Pedrarias was greedy and jealous of Balboa's success. He sent his soldiers to torture the natives and steal their gold.

Disturbed at the treatment of people who had become his friends, Balboa decided to leave Darien in 1515. Pedrarias refused to give his permission, but Balboa left anyway. He and 200 men traveled to a village of friendly Indians to prepare for another journey to the Pacific Ocean and a trip to Peru.

1. Why do you think Pedrarias didn't want Balboa to leave Darien?

_____

_____

_____

_____

_____

After King Ferdinand died, Pedrarias feared that he would be recalled to Spain and punished for his cruel treatment of the natives. To draw attention away from his own misdeeds, he sent Francisco Pizarro to escort Balboa to Acla where he was arrested, convicted of treason, and beheaded.

Balboa recommended that a channel be cut through the isthmus to connect the Atlantic and Pacific Oceans. However, that plan wasn't carried out for more than 400 years when the Panama Canal was built by the United States.

Panama has honored Balboa by naming its monetary unit, the balboa, after him.

Name: _____ Date: _____

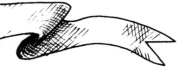

Preparing for a Sea Voyage

The year is 1500. You are the captain of a ship about to set sail for the New World. It's your job to make a list of supplies for the voyage. The trip is expected to take two to three months. You have a crew of 35. Keep in mind that the ship has no electricity or refrigeration, and you can't include anything that has not been invented yet.

What will you and your crew need for a long, dangerous voyage? Remember, the ship will not make any stops along the way to resupply the crew with food, tools, weapons, water, clothing, medicine, or anything else.

1. Write your list below. Be as thorough and specific as possible.

_____   _____   _____

_____   _____   _____

_____   _____   _____

_____   _____   _____

_____   _____   _____

_____   _____   _____

_____   _____   _____

_____   _____   _____

_____   _____   _____

2. Compare your list with a partner. Add important items you may have forgotten. What was the most important item you forgot to include?

_____

3. Name five things that were invented after 1500 that would have been useful on your voyage.

_____   _____   _____

_____   _____

Name: _____ Date: _____

Meet Amerigo Vespucci

Born: 1454 in Florence, Italy
Died: 1512

Since people believed Christopher Columbus was the first European to visit the New World, why weren't the continents named North and South Columbia? Columbus never realized he discovered a New World. When he died, he still thought he had found a sea route to the East Indies.

Like Columbus, Amerigo Vespucci was Italian. As a young man, he had an interest in mathematics, cartography, and astronomy.

Amerigo Vespucci was the Italian navigator for whom the continents of North and South America were named.

1. Use a dictionary: What is cartography?_____

_____

_____

2. Use a dictionary: What is astronomy? _____

_____

3. How would knowledge of mathematics, cartography, and astronomy help prepare a person to become an explorer?

_____

_____

Vespucci worked for bankers in Florence, Italy, and was sent to Spain to look after the bank's business there. While in Spain, he made his first voyage, not as the captain, but as a navigator.

4. Use a dictionary: What is a navigator? _____

_____

In 1499, the crew explored the coast of South America to the mouth of the Amazon River. By observing the conjunction of Mars and the moon, Vespucci was able to calculate how far west he had traveled.

5. How old was Vespucci when he made his first voyage to the New World?

_____

Name: _____ Date: _____

How Vespucci Became Famous

Vespucci's second voyage in 1501 was on a Portuguese ship. The voyage across the Atlantic Ocean took 64 days. Again the crew explored the coast of South America to within 400 miles of its southern tip, Tierra del Fuego.

While on this voyage, Vespucci wrote long letters to a friend describing his travels. He was the first to realize that this was a separate continent, not part of Asia. Although he did not captain the ship, his accounts of what they saw, maps of the areas they explored, and ability to write were what eventually made him famous.

In his letters, Vespucci described the culture and people he met in the New World. He included information about the natives' diet, religion, family life, marriage, society, and children. His letters were published in many languages and became very popular.

1. Why do you think people in Europe were interested in reading Vespucci's letters?

   _____

   _____

   _____

On his third and final voyage, Vespucci contracted malaria and died after he returned to Spain in 1512.

Vespucci did not name the continents of the New World after himself. That was done by a German cartographer, Martin Waldseemuller, who was drawing a new, updated world map. He had read of Vespucci's travels and decided to honor him on his map. He printed and sold his map with the name America on the southern continent of the New World.

Another mapmaker, Gerardus Mercator, was the first to include North and South America on a world map he produced in 1538.

Think About It: If Waldseemuller had decided to name the continent Vespucci, we might now live in the United States of Vespucci!

2. Some accounts say Vespucci made four voyages to the New World. Why do you think the "facts" in some history books are different than in others, not only for Amerigo Vespucci, but also for other events that occurred in the past?

   _____

   _____

   _____

Check It Out:
Forgotten Voyager: The Story of Amerigo Vespucci by Ann Fitzgerald Alper

Name: _____ Date: _____

Meet John Cabot

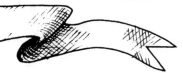

Born: about 1450 in Genoa, Italy
Died: 1499

John Cabot moved to England in 1484, seeking an opportunity to explore and obtain the fabulous riches of China. Like Columbus and others of his time, John Cabot thought there must be a sea route to the riches of Asia by sailing west instead of east.

After being turned down by merchants in Spain and Portugal, Cabot received a charter from Henry VII of England, giving him the right to discover new lands. The king provided only one small ship (less than 70 feet long) called the *Matthew* and a crew of 18. Cabot and his crew were forced to turn back during their first voyage in 1496 due to bad weather and lack of food.

Cabot sailed from England on a second voyage on May 2, 1497, taking a route much further to the north than Columbus had taken. On June 24, they sighted land somewhere in Newfoundland.

Although John Cabot sounds like an English name, he was actually Italian. He lived for a time in Venice and worked as a trader in what we now call the Middle East. In Italy, he was known as Giovanni Caboto.

1. Counting the day they left and the day they arrived, how many days did this voyage take?

_____

Cabot, like Columbus, was convinced he had found an island off the coast of Asia and called it "new found land."

2. Do you think "Newfoundland" was a good name? Why or why not? _____

_____

When he returned to England two months later, he didn't bring any riches, silk, or spices, but he had made a map of part of the North American coast. He also reported that one only had to lower a basket over the side of the boat, and it would be filled with fish. King Henry agreed to finance another voyage. Cabot's ship was joined by four other ships provided by merchants who hoped to cash in on what they thought was a new route to the Orient. They left in May, 1498. One of the merchant ships returned to England for repairs, but the other four, with John Cabot as captain, were never seen again.

Check It Out:
The Travels of John and Sebastian Cabot by Joanne Mattern
John Cabot and Son by David Goodnough

Name: _____ Date: _____

A Charter From the King

Part of the charter granted to John Cabot by Henry VII reads as follows:

"Be known that we have given ... to John Cabot, citizen of Venice, and to Lewis, Sebastian and Sancio, sons of the said John ... full and free authority... to sail to all parts, regions and coasts of the eastern, western and northern sea ... to find, discover and investigate whatsoever islands, countries, regions or provinces of heathens and infidels, in whatsoever part of the world placed, which before this time were unknown to all Christians."

1. Summarize what you think King Henry meant in the first part of this charter. Use a dictionary if any of the words are unclear.

   _____

   _____

   _____

"John and his sons ... may conquer, occupy and possess whatsoever such towns, castles, cities and islands by them thus discovered ... as our vassals and governors ... acquiring for us the dominion, title and jurisdiction of the same [places] ... so discovered ... [All] gains and revenues accruing from this voyage ... [they] shall be bound [upon arriving in] our port of Bristol ... to pay to us, either in goods or money, the fifth part of the whole capital gained ... that they may bring back with them from those places newly discovered."

2. According to this section of the charter, what percentage of the amount earned would be due to the king?

   _____

"And further we have granted ... that all mainlands, islands, towns, cities, castles and other places whatsoever discovered by them, however numerous they may happen to be, may not be frequented or visited by any other subjects of ours ... without the license of ... John and his sons ... on pain of loss as well of the ships or vessels daring to sail to these places discovered ..."

3. What rights does this section of the charter give to John Cabot?

   _____

   _____

4. If you had been John Cabot, would you have wanted to accept this charter from the king? Why or why not?

   _____

   _____

Name: _____ Date: _____

Searching for Wealth

Vasco da Gama discovered a sea route around the tip of Africa to the East during a two-year voyage (1497–1499). However, this involved a long and dangerous journey.

1. On another sheet of paper, write a short report about the voyage of Vasco da Gama around Africa.

By the early 1500s, explorers realized that what Columbus had discovered were not islands off the coast of Asia, but rather islands near a large, unknown landmass that lay between Europe and the East. However, no one yet realized the enormous size of the North and South American continents. Rather than seeing the new lands as a great opportunity, many believed they were only an obstacle, blocking the way to where they really wanted to go.

2. Why do you think people were more interested in reaching China than they were in exploring a new land?

_____

_____

_____

_____

_____

3. If you had been a king or queen in 1500, and someone asked you to provide ships, crew, and money to finance a voyage in search of a shorter route to China, would you have agreed? Why or why not?

_____

_____

_____

_____

_____

4. If you had been asked to join the crew of a ship in 1500 on a voyage to discover a route to China across unknown oceans, would you have accepted? Why or why not?

_____

_____

_____

_____

_____

Name: _____ Date: _____

Meet Sebastian Cabot

Born: about 1476 in Italy
Died: 1557

Like his father, Sebastian Cabot began his career as a mapmaker. Sebastian claimed he had sailed with his father to North America in 1497, but evidence of that is slim. Many other claims he made during his life have also been questioned by historians. Some of his actions have led to the belief that he was not a very honest or honorable person.

By convincing King Henry VII of England that he could find a water passageway through North America to the East, Cabot received two ships and support from the king. In 1508, he sailed in search of that shortcut. Sebastian took a northern route like his father had.

After his father, John, was lost at sea in 1499, Sebastian Cabot also sailed in search of an alternate route to the East.

Cabot reached the coast of Labrador and sailed north as far as Greenland. Finding ice floes even in the summer convinced Cabot to sail west. There he discovered a waterway that led inland. Cabot followed the waterway (Hudson Strait) to a large body of water (Hudson Bay). Cabot thought he had discovered the passage he had sought.

1. Locate Greenland, Hudson Strait, and Hudson Bay on a world map. If he had continued sailing west, would Cabot have found a water passage to Asia?

   _____

2. Cabot's crew, cold and tired of the long voyage, threatened mutiny. What does *mutiny* mean?

   _____

   _____

3. If you had been Sebastian Cabot, what would you have done?

   _____

   _____

   _____

Cabot agreed to return to the main coast and head south, hoping to find another passage in a warmer area. They returned to England after exploring the eastern coast of North America as far south as Cape Hatteras, North Carolina.

Name: _____ Date: _____

The Search Continues

By the time Sebastian Cabot returned to England in 1509, Henry VII had died. Henry VIII, the new king, had no interest in financing Cabot for another voyage. Cabot moved to Spain where he made maps for the Spanish navy and became a naval aide to King Ferdinand. He tried to persuade the king to sponsor another voyage, but the king died in 1516 before Cabot could convince him.

The new king of Spain, King Charles I, would not agree to Cabot's request. Instead, he appointed Cabot as Pilot Major (chief navigator) of Spain. Cabot supervised other explorers and recorded their discoveries on his maps. Although this was a high-paying, important position, Cabot wasn't satisfied. While employed by the king of Spain, he continued secretly to try to win support from the king of England.

In 1526, Cabot finally received permission from Charles I for another voyage. His instructions were to follow Magellan's route to the Spice Islands of the East Indies. He sailed with four ships to South America where he heard reports of vast wealth from natives in the area. Cabot abandoned his mission and began an unsuccessful search for gold. During the four wasted years of his voyage, one ship sank, many of his crew were killed by hostile natives, and some of his men mutinied and were hanged.

Not having found any great treasures in South America, Cabot returned to Spain in 1530. His officers charged him with abusing his crew and disobeying orders. He was arrested, found guilty, and sentenced to banishment in Africa for three years. King Charles pardoned him, and Cabot resumed his position as Pilot Major. He spent the next few years as a mapmaker, completing a new engraved map of the world published in 1544. During that time, he continued to maintain contact with the English government, hoping for something better.

In 1547, King Edward VI placed him in charge of England's maritime affairs and appointed him Pilot Major of England. He became governor of the Muscovy Company of Merchant Adventurers, an English trading organization dedicated to finding a northern passage to China.

Although he accomplished much in his life, Cabot never achieved the wealth he desired nor discovered the sea route to China.

1. Some historians claim Sebastian Cabot was a scoundrel. From what you've learned, do you agree or disagree? Explain your answer in a paragraph on another sheet of paper.

Check It Out:
The Travels of John and Sebastian Cabot by Joanne Mattern
John and Sebastian Cabot by Henry Kurtz

Name: _____ Date: _____

Magellan Circumnavigates the Earth

In August of 1519, Ferdinand Magellan sailed from Seville, Spain, with five ships. Although he died before completing the voyage, the *Victoria,* one of his ships, became the first to sail around the world.

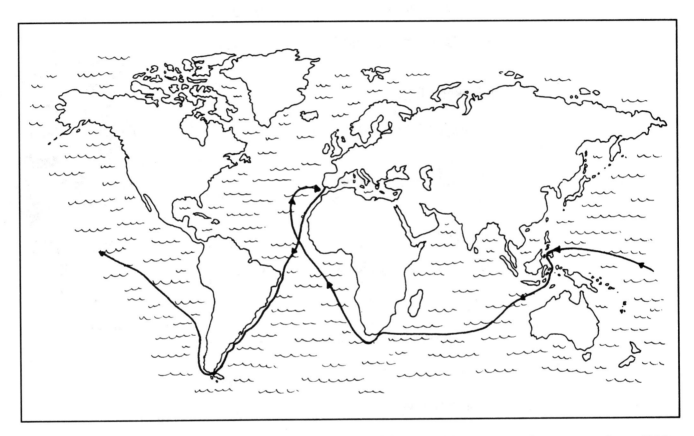

Use the Internet or other reference sources and the map above to answer the questions. Write your answers on another sheet of paper.

1. What does *circumnavigate* mean?
2. Why did Ferdinand Magellan make his voyage?
3. Where and how did Magellan die?
4. What continents did Magellan's ships visit on the way?
5. What did Magellan's route prove beyond all doubt?

Check It Out:

Ferdinand Magellan and the First Voyage Around the World by Jim Gallagher
Around the World in One Hundred Years: From Henry the Navigator to Magellan by Jean Fritz

Name: _____ Date: _____

Let's Review

Matching.

_____ 1. What was the name of John Cabot's ship?

_____ 2. Who was Leif Erikson's father?

_____ 3. Which of Columbus's ships was the largest?

_____ 4. Where was Leif Erikson born?

_____ 5. What did Leif Erikson call the land he discovered?

_____ 6. Route used by the first people to come to North America

_____ 7. His real name was Giovanni Caboto.

_____ 8. His descriptive letters made him famous.

_____ 9. This king gave John Cabot a charter.

_____ 10. First European to visit North America

_____ 11. First European to see the Pacific Ocean

_____ 12. Country where Columbus was born

_____ 13. Country where Balboa was born

_____ 14. Appointed Pilot Major of England and Spain

A. Bering land bridge

B. John Cabot

C. *Matthew*

D. Leif Erikson

E. Iceland

F. *Santa Maria*

G. Henry VII

H. Erik the Red

I. Spain

J. Vinland

K. Sebastian Cabot

L. Italy

M. Amerigo Vespucci

N. Vasco de Balboa

15. Which of these men do you admire most: Leif Erikson, Christopher Columbus, Amerigo Vespucci, Vasco de Balboa, John Cabot, or Sebastian Cabot? Give at least three reasons for your answer.

_____

_____

_____

_____

Name: _____ Date: _____

Meet Juan Ponce de León

Born: about 1460 in León, Spain
Died: 1521

As a boy, Juan Ponce de León was a page in the royal court of Aragon. Later, he served in the army during campaigns against the Muslims in southern Spain.

Ponce de León sailed with Columbus on his second voyage to the New World in 1493. Instead of returning to Spain with Columbus, de León remained in Santo Domingo. He helped the governor subdue a native insurrection in 1504. For his services, he was appointed provincial governor of eastern Hispaniola.

Juan Ponce de León, better known simply as Ponce de León, was the first European to visit Florida.

Rumors of gold on the island of Borinquen (Puerto Rico) prompted de León to lead a group of settlers to the island in 1509 where they founded the city of Capara (near San Juan). He became the governor of Puerto Rico, but in 1511, King Ferdinand ordered Diego Columbus to replace de León because he was so ruthless in his treatment of Native Americans. By then de León was already a wealthy man.

1. If you had the choice, would you have returned to Spain with your wealth or remained in the New World seeking more adventures and riches? Explain your reasons.

_____

_____

_____

_____

De León heard rumors of Bimini, an island possibly in the Bahamas, where a fountain of youth flowed, surrounded by gold and silver. He received permission to conquer and settle Bimini if he could find it.

De León sailed from Puerto Rico on March 3, 1513, with three ships. They stopped on several islands, but none held the mythical fountain of youth or any great treasures.

2. Why do you think anyone would believe such incredible rumors?

_____

_____

_____

25

Name: _____ Date: _____

A Frustrating Search

Finally, on Easter Sunday, de León landed on the coast of Florida near what is now St. Augustine. He called it the land of flowers. At the time, he thought Florida was another island.

1. Find Puerto Rico, Cuba, the Bahamas, and Florida on a map. Why do you think de León thought Florida was also an island?

_____

_____

_____

De León and his men searched the area for gold, silver, pearls, and the fountain of youth, but again found nothing. He sailed south around the Florida Keys and up the west coast of Florida near Sanibel Island. They stopped to replenish their food and named these islands the Tortugas for the many turtles they found. From there, they returned to Puerto Rico.

The king of Spain knighted de León and appointed him governor of Florida, but first he was commanded to subdue the Carib tribe, which was raiding Puerto Rico. These Native Americans were fierce fighters, able to cross the Caribbean in huge canoes.

In 1521, de León resumed his search for the fountain of youth. He returned to Florida with two ships carrying 200 colonists and many domestic animals. They landed on the west coast of Florida where they were attacked by the Calusa. De León was wounded with a poison arrow. The colonists returned to the ships and sailed back to Cuba where De León died of his wounds.

Ponce de León was buried in San Juan, Puerto Rico. These words were written on his grave: Beneath this stone lie the bones of the valiant Lion (León means lion) whose deeds surpassed the greatness of his name.

2. Do you agree with this description of Ponce de León's life? Why or why not?

_____

_____

_____

_____

Check It Out:
Juan Ponce de León and the Search for the Fountain of Youth by Dan Harmon
The Travels of Juan Ponce de León by Deborah Crisfield

Name: _____ Date: _____

The Fountain of Youth

Ponce de León wasn't the first person to search for the mythical fountain of youth, nor was he the last to spend much time and effort searching for what didn't exist. He heard stories that claimed the fountain of youth flowed with water that cured illness and granted the drinker eternal youth. Other rumors reported much gold and silver surrounded the magical fountain.

1. If you discovered a fountain of youth, would you drink from it? Why or why not? Give several specific reasons for your answer.

_____

_____

_____

_____

2. What would be the advantages of never growing older than you are now?

_____

_____

_____

_____

3. What would be the disadvantages of never growing older, especially if you were the only one who had eternal youth?

_____

_____

_____

_____

4. If you found the fountain of youth, would you share your discovery with others or keep it a secret? Give reasons for your answer. Be very specific.

_____

_____

_____

_____

Name: _____ Date: _____

In the News

Newspaper headlines are brief summaries of the most important point of an article. Headlines must be brief, to the point, and grab the reader's attention. Read the headlines of all the stories on the front page of any newspaper.

Write newspaper headlines for the events below. None of your headlines may contain more than six words.

1. Leif Erikson left Greenland and sailed to an unknown land where he saw large salmon in the water, seabirds in the air, and many plants and trees. He named it Vinland.

   _____

2. The Italian navigator, Christopher Columbus, received financial backing from King Ferdinand and Queen Isabella of Spain to sail west in search of a new route to China.

   _____

3. Vasco Núñez de Balboa crossed the thick jungles and swamps of the Isthmus of Panama. After a long, difficult journey, he became the first European to see the Pacific Ocean. He named it the South Sea.

   _____

4. Ferdinand Magellan sailed around the southern tip of South America and discovered a route to the Spice Islands of the East Indies.

   _____

5. During a difficult two-year voyage, Vasco da Gama discovered a sea route around the southern tip of Africa that allowed others to travel by sea to the East.

   _____

6. Sebastian Cabot returned to Spain empty-handed after a wasted four-year voyage. His officers accused him of mistreating the crew and not following orders. Cabot was convicted and sentenced to banishment in Africa.

   _____

7. Juan Ponce de León of Spain searched for many years, visited many islands in the New World, and finally, at the age of 102, discovered the fountain of youth. He feels great but forgot where he found it.

   _____

Name: _____   Date: _____

Meet Hernan Cortés

Born: 1485 in Medellin, Spain
Died: 1547

Hernan Cortés left Spain in 1504 when he was about 19 years old after studying law for a short time at the University of Salamanca. He served as a clerk to Diego Velázquez during the campaign to conquer and settle Cuba.

As the European population of Cuba grew, Velázquez, now governor, realized there wasn't enough land or slave labor on the island. Expeditions sent to the Yucatán Peninsula between 1516 and 1518 found indications of a wealthy civilization. Velázquez decided to send Cortés on an expedition to explore, trade, and search for Christian captives.

The conquest of the Aztec empire by Hernan Cortés gave Spain a base of power that spread rapidly throughout Central and South America.

Before Cortés left, Velázquez began to suspect that Cortés was not loyal and cancelled his commission. Cortés ignored him, recruited soldiers, and sailed to Mexico in 1519.

Cortés founded his own city, Veracruz, in the name of the king of Spain and made himself its leader. Fearing that some of his soldiers might rebel, he burned his fleet so they could not leave.

1. If you had been one of Cortés's soldiers, how would you have felt about that?

    _____

    _____

    _____

Cortés then sent word to King Charles I of Spain, asking the king to confirm him as leader of the settlement and seeking permission to lead a "just war" against the ruler of the people of Mexico who had "ungodly ways." He also described the wealth of the Aztecs and his desire to claim it for Christianity and the king. Without waiting for a reply, he set out overland.

2. Do you think Cortés really believed what he told the king? Why or why not?

    _____

    _____

    _____

    _____

Name: _____ Date: _____

Cortés Meets Montezuma

With the help of translators, Cortés recruited people from other tribes who were hostile to the Aztecs. After a 250-mile march, they arrived at the capital city of Tenochtitlán.

1. Considering they had never seen white-skinned, bearded men, metal armor, or horses, how do you think the Aztecs felt when Cortés and his army arrived?

   _____

   _____

   _____

   _____

   _____

   _____

The Aztecs believed Cortés fulfilled a prophesy that a descendent of a white-skinned, bearded god, Quetzalcóatl, would return from the east to rule the Aztecs. At first, they welcomed the Spaniards with lavish gifts.

Although their meeting started in a friendly manner, relations between the Spaniards and Aztecs soon changed. Perhaps Montezuma realized that Cortés was not a god. Perhaps Cortés feared they would become human sacrifices or was greedy for more wealth. For whatever reason, Cortés seized Montezuma, the Aztec emperor, and held him prisoner. The Aztecs gathered treasures for ransom.

Cortés learned that Velázquez had sent soldiers to return him to Cuba. He captured their leader and persuaded most of the soldiers to join him.

2. Why do you think soldiers who had been sent to capture Cortés changed their minds and joined him?

   _____

   _____

   _____

   _____

30

Name: _____ Date: _____

Conquest of the Aztecs

When he returned to Tenochtitlán, Cortés discovered his soldiers had provoked an uprising by killing many Aztecs during a religious ceremony.

Cortés convinced Montezuma to speak to the crowd to try to restore order. Considering him a traitor, the Aztecs threw stones at Montezuma. He was struck in the head and died three days later. A full-scale rebellion began. More than half the Spaniards were killed as they retreated from the city.

1. If you had been Montezuma, held prisoner by Cortés and forced to speak to your people to try to make them stop their rebellion, what would you have said?

_____

_____

_____

_____

Cortés reinforced his army with people from tribes who were enemies of the Aztecs and returned to Tenochtitlán in 1521. They blockaded the city, cutting off the supply of food and water. After three months, an outbreak of smallpox further weakened the defenders, and Cortés finally pushed his way into the city. The Spanish army razed the city until hardly any trace of the Aztecs remained. Mexico City was built on the ruins.

Cortés hoped his success would persuade the king to absolve him of his rebellion against Velázquez. King Charles I named Cortés governor of New Spain in 1523 and granted him many riches.

2. Define *rebellion:* _____

_____

_____

3. What does *absolve* mean? _____

_____

_____

Cortés led another expedition to Honduras in 1524. By then, even the king feared Cortés was too ambitious and recalled him to Spain. He gave Cortés the title Marquis of Oaxaca but removed him as governor. When Cortés returned to Mexico, his activities were checked, his property and rights denied, and his popularity declined.

Name: _____ Date: _____

Was Cortés a Hero?

Cortés continued exploring. He discovered the peninsula of Baja California in 1536. When the king granted Francisco Coronado the right to search for the Seven Cities of Cíbola, Cortés returned to Spain to complain. The king ignored Cortés's demands to restore his rights and property. Eventually, Cortés retired to a small estate near Seville, Spain, where he died.

By conquering and destroying a magnificent civilization, Hernan Cortés gave Spain a power base in Mexico that lasted until the nineteenth century. To gain his ends, he killed and enslaved thousands of Native Americans.

Cortés claimed his actions were for the benefit of the king and Christianity. Others believe his principal purpose seemed to be to win fame and wealth for himself.

1. Which point of view do you believe? Explain why.

   _____

   _____

   _____

   _____

   _____

   _____

2. Some people say "the end justifies the means." In the case of Cortés, do you agree or disagree? Write your reasons.

   _____

   _____

   _____

   _____

   _____

   _____

   _____

Check It Out:
Hernando Cortés and the Conquest of Mexico by Gina De Angelis
The Travels of Hernan Cortés by Deborah Crisfield

Name: _____ Date: _____

Meet Francisco Pizarro

Born: about 1475 in Trujillo, Spain
Died: 1541

Francisco Pizarro arrived in Hispaniola in 1502. He joined an expedition to Columbia in 1509. While serving under Vasco de Balboa, he became his chief lieutenant during the march across Panama to the Pacific Ocean. Later, Pizarro became a captain for Pedrarias, the governor of Panama, who had Pizarro arrest Balboa for treason.

While in Panama, Pizarro heard rumors of a rich and powerful empire located further south. He and a longtime friend, Diego de Almagro, organized an expedition to explore and search for gold in 1524. Bad weather and hostile natives soon ended their quest. A second expedition in 1526 also ended in failure.

Although he started life in poverty, Francisco Pizarro gained fabulous wealth before he died.

Pizarro returned to Spain and received permission from King Charles I to conquer the Incas and become the governor of Peru. He raised an army and returned to Peru in 1532 with about 180 men.

Pizarro and his soldiers sailed along the coast of South America. They traveled inland at one point and raided a village where they seized gold and learned more about the riches of the people of Peru. The impenetrable jungles forced them back to their ships, and they continued sailing south.

At the city of Tumbes, a northern outpost of the Incan empire, the Spaniards found out that the Incas were engaged in a civil war between two brothers, Atahualpa and Huascar, who both wanted to rule the empire.

Learning that Atahualpa was in the city of Cajamarca, Pizarro and his troops marched on. Even though Atahualpa must have heard rumors of the atrocities Pizarro committed, he sent guides with gifts who helped them along the route. They told Pizarro that Atahualpa had an army of 40,000 warriors. When he reached Cajamarca, Pizarro found a clean city with piped water and sewage and irrigation systems.

1. Use reference sources to learn more about the Incan culture. Write a short report on one aspect of Incan society.

Name: _____ Date: _____

Pizarro Uses Treachery to Defeat the Incas

Pizarro sent Hernando de Soto and 20 men to meet with Atahualpa. The Spaniards on horseback in gleaming armor must have been an impressive sight to the Incas. De Soto told Atahualpa that Pizarro had 30,000 men in camp and another 10,000 armed men surrounding the city.

1. From his scouts and spies, Atahualpa must have known the truth about how few soldiers were with Pizarro. Why do you think he did not try to defeat them?

    _____

    _____

    _____

    _____

Pizarro persuaded Atahualpa to attend a huge feast with his nobles. He arrived with thousands of Incas. A priest greeted Atahualpa and gave a long sermon using translators. He told the Incas they must pledge allegiance to the great king and queen of Spain, give up their pagan gods, and follow Christianity. He handed Atahualpa a Bible, but the Inca chief threw it to the ground.

2. How would you feel if aliens came to your town, said you must pledge loyalty to rulers on another planet you had never heard of, give up all of your beliefs, and do everything their way from now on?

    _____

    _____

    _____

    _____

Pizarro's troops, previously hidden, surrounded the Incas, and with the aid of horses and cannon, slaughtered most of the guests. They captured Atahualpa and held him for ransom.

Atahualpa agreed to fill one large room with gold and two smaller rooms with silver in exchange for his release—over 13,000 pounds of gold and 26,000 pounds of silver, which would be worth $100 million in today's money.

Pizarro accepted the offer, but after the ransom was paid, he refused to release Atahualpa. The Spaniards looted the city, torturing and killing thousands. They forced many to become slaves. Fearing Atahualpa would rally the support of the Incas to fight the Spaniards, Pizarro had him executed on August 29, 1533.

Name: _____ Date: _____

More Treachery

Pizarro supported Manco Capac to succeed Atahualpa as ruler of the Incas. The Spaniards marched to the city of Cusco where they defeated the remainder of Atahualpa's followers and looted the city. Pizarro allowed Manco to rule in Cusco as a puppet leader, but he, himself, actually ruled from Lima, the new capital of Peru.

1. What does "puppet leader" mean?

   _____

   _____

   _____

   _____

Pizarro established a system of forced labor among the native people. Spanish abuses finally convinced Manco to lead a revolt, but he was unsuccessful.

Conflict occurred between Pizarro and his partner, Diego de Almagro, who claimed Cusco for himself. During the power struggle, Almagro was killed. Almagro's followers took revenge by assassinating Pizarro in his palace in Lima in 1541.

Fact or Fiction?

Can you separate fact from fiction? Use reference sources to find the answers. Circle Fact or Fiction for each statement below.

1. Fact or Fiction: Francisco Pizarro's parents were never married.

2. Fact or Fiction: Pizarro could not read or write.

3. Fact or Fiction: Pizarro was over 50 years old when he conquered the Incas of Peru.

4. Fact or Fiction: When Pizarro returned to Spain to seek permission from King Charles I for an expedition to Peru, he was thrown in jail because of an unpaid debt.

On another sheet of paper, compare Cortés's conquest of the Aztecs to Pizarro's conquest of the Incas. Explain how the two conquests were similar and how they were different.

Check It Out:
Pizarro and the Conquest of the Incan Empire by Richard Worth
Travels of Francisco Pizarro by Lara Rice Bergen

Name: _____   Date: _____

Meet Francisco Vasquez de Coronado

Born: about 1510 in Salamanca, Spain
Died: 1554 in Mexico City

Born to a noble family in Spain, Francisco Coronado became friendly with Antonio de Mendoza. When Mendoza was appointed viceroy to New Spain (Mexico) in 1535, Coronado traveled with him. In 1538, Coronado helped put down a rebellion of African slaves.

A year later, Mendoza appointed Coronado as governor of New Galicia, a province in western Mexico. From Cabeza de Vaca and Frey Marcos de Niza, they heard stories of natives who wore emeralds and gold in the Seven Golden Cities of Cíbola. Of course, Coronado and Mendoza were very interested.

Although he never found the fabled Seven Cities of Cíbola, Francisco Coronado established Spain's claim to a large portion of what later became the southwestern United States.

From the time the first Spaniards ventured to the New World, they had heard stories and legends of fabulous wealth, fountains of youth, and cities of gold. In almost every case, the stories were nothing but rumors or lies. But every once in a while, someone like Hernan Cortés or Francisco Pizarro would discover the truth behind the stories. That was enough incentive to lure thousands into leading or joining expeditions in the belief that they would be among the lucky few.

1. Would you be willing to join an expedition searching for a lost gold mine or buried treasure? Why or why not?

_____

_____

_____

_____

2. Describe how you would feel if you were one of the lucky ones to discover a great treasure.

_____

_____

_____

_____

_____

In Search of the Seven Cities of Cíbola

Mendoza, Coronado, and other investors contributed what amounted to several million dollars in today's money to finance the expedition. In 1540, Coronado set off with 340 Spaniards, 300 native allies, and 1,000 Native American and African slaves. They took along herds of cattle, pigs, and sheep.

There was trouble from the beginning. They were slowed down by too many people, too much baggage, and the herds of animals they took for food. A smaller force continued. By the time they had traveled 300 miles, Coronado began receiving reports that the stories of the Seven Cities of Cíbola were false. That news must have been a terrible blow to Coronado who had invested much of his wife's money and his reputation in the expedition.

1. If you had been Coronado, would you have continued? Why or why not?

   _____

   _____

   _____

Part of Coronado's expedition continued to march north into Arizona and then northeast to New Mexico, hungry, thirsty, and suffering as they crossed the deserts. There they found the first of the seven cities, but it was not a fabulous city of gold. What they found were the simple pueblos of the Zuni and natives willing to fight to defend their homes. Coronado conquered the Zuni there and in other areas, but nowhere did he find any great cities of gold.

Over the winter, Coronado heard stories from an Indian slave of Quivira, a rich city to the northeast. With 30 men, Coronado followed his guide to central Kansas where they found the Wichita people living in tepees. When the slave confessed he had invented the story, Coronado had him executed and returned to his base in New Mexico.

2. How would you have felt if you had been Coronado?

   _____

   _____

   _____

3. What would you have done?

   _____

   _____

   _____

   _____

Name: _____   Date: _____

What Did Coronado Really Discover?

In the meantime, Coronado had sent various groups off to explore the area. One group, led by Garcia López de Cárdenas, discovered the spectacular Grand Canyon. Another group found the fertile Rio Grande valley. Melchor Díaz discovered that lower California was a peninsula, not an island. Upon reaching the banks of the Colorado River, he became the first European to travel by land from Mexico to California.

During his journey to Kansas, Coronado and his group were the first Europeans to see and describe the great herds of American bison. They explored along the Kansas and Arkansas Rivers. In all, they had traveled nearly 3,000 miles from Mexico to a point approximately in the center of what is today the United States. All of this land they claimed for Spain.

1. Coronado and his expeditions traveled though what later became California, New Mexico, Arizona, Texas, Oklahoma, Arkansas, and Kansas. Label these states on the map.

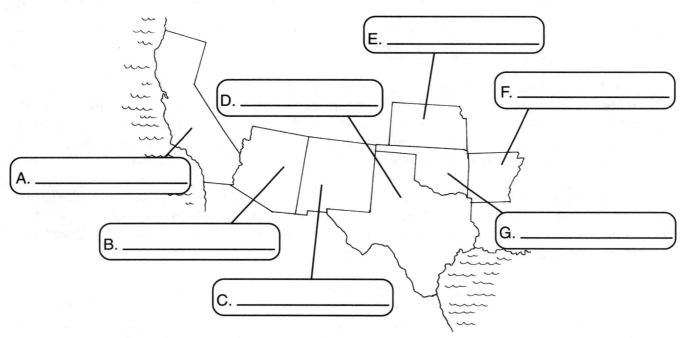

Coronado was badly injured in a fall from a horse. A fortuneteller in Spain had predicted he would become rich, famous, and powerful but would eventually fall from a horse and never recover. Although some of his officers wanted to continue to explore, Coronado decided to return to Mexico. Only about 100 of his men returned with him.

Coronado remained governor until 1544, when he was charged with corruption, negligence, and cruelty to the Native Americans. He retired to Mexico City where he died in 1554.

Check It Out:
From Coronado to Escabante: The Explorers of the Spanish Southwest by John Miller Morris
Coronado: Dreamer in Golden Armor by William Jay Jacobs

Name: _____ Date: _____

Meet Hernando de Soto

Born: about 1500 in Barcarrota, Spain
Died: 1542

After spending several years as an aide to the governor of Panama, Hernando de Soto joined Francisco Pizarro in 1530 on the coast of Ecuador and became his second-in-command.

Pizarro led the Spanish army south to Caxamarca, Peru. He and de Soto lured the Inca emperor into a trap and held him hostage until they received millions of dollars in gold in ransom. Then Pizarro executed the emperor.

De Soto returned to Spain in 1536, rich and famous, but he wanted more. He wanted power. After marrying the daughter of the governor of Panama, de Soto asked King Charles I of Spain to appoint him as governor of Columbia and Ecuador. The king feared Pizarro and de Soto would join together and set up a powerful empire of their own in South America.

Like thousands of other Spanish soldiers, Hernando de Soto came to the New World in search of gold.

1. Knowing what kind of men they were, do you think King Charles was right to worry that Pizarro and de Soto might join and set up their own empire? Why or why not?

   _____

   _____

   _____

Instead, King Charles appointed de Soto governor of Cuba and Florida and gave him the authority to explore and conquer Florida for Spain. Like others, de Soto had heard rumors of cities of gold and a fountain of youth hidden in Florida.

2. Do you think this appointment made de Soto happy? Why or why not?

   _____

   _____

   _____

Check It Out:
De Soto by Matthew G. Grant
Hernando de Soto by Abbott Chrisman

Name: _____   Date: _____

De Soto as Governor of Florida

In 1538, de Soto sailed from Spain with his wife and a large army. When they arrived in Havana, Cuba, de Soto set his wife up as governor. With 1,000 soldiers, de Soto sailed to Tampa Bay, Florida.

1. Why do you think de Soto appointed his wife as governor while he was gone?

_____

_____

In Tampa Bay, they found a Spaniard, Juan Ortiz, living with Native Americans. Ortiz had come to Florida 10 years earlier, been captured, and had lived with them since. Ortiz became their guide and helped them make peace with the natives.

However, that peace did not last. De Soto and his army marched off to conquer the natives and search for gold and the fountain of youth. De Soto made enemies by stealing crops, burning villages, and enslaving the people.

2. If you had been living in Florida at the time, how would you have felt about de Soto and his army?

_____

_____

_____

While searching for gold, de Soto and his soldiers explored much of what later became the southeastern United States, including parts of Florida, North and South Carolina, Tennessee, Georgia, Alabama, Mississippi, Arkansas, and Texas.

Along the way, many men died of sickness, in attacks, and from insect and snake bites. After a battle at Movilla, a large Choctaw city, de Soto lost many more men. Most of their equipment and horses were gone too. His men urged him to return home, but de Soto refused to give up his dreams of wealth and power.

3. If you had been one of his soldiers, far from home, marching through unknown country for several years, what would you have said to de Soto?

_____

_____

_____

In 1541, de Soto and his group became the first Europeans to see the Mississippi River. In the spring of 1542, de Soto fell ill and died. His aide buried him in the river to keep his death a secret from the natives.

Name: _____ Date: _____

Let's Review

Matching

_____ 1. God of the Aztecs

_____ 2. Aztec capital city

_____ 3. Inca capital city

_____ 4. Inca emperor

_____ 5. Conquered the Aztecs

_____ 6. City founded by Cortés

_____ 7. Conquered the Incas

_____ 8. Searched for fountain of youth

_____ 9. Aztec emperor

_____ 10. "Turtle islands"

_____ 11. Means "conqueror"

_____ 12. Searched for the Seven Cities of Cíbola

_____ 13. Country of the Incas

_____ 14. Found in Cíbola

_____ 15. Explored by Coronado

A. Peru

B. Francisco Pizarro

C. Montezuma

D. Pueblos

E. Tenochtitlán

F. Hernan Cortés

G. Ponce de León

H. Tortugas

I. Quetzalcóatl

J. Atahualpa

K. Veracruz

L. Cajamarca

M. New Mexico and Texas

N. Francisco Coronado

O. Conquistador

16. Which of these men do you admire **least**: Ponce de León, Hernan Cortés, Francisco Pizarro, or Francisco Coronado? Give at least three reasons for your answer.

_____

_____

_____

_____

_____

Name: _____ Date: _____

Interview an Explorer

You are a journalist with a once-in-a-lifetime opportunity to interview Hernan Cortés, Francisco Pizarro, Ponce de León, or Francisco Coronado for your newspaper. Which of these explorers would you interview? Explain your reasons for selecting that man.

_____

_____

_____

To conduct a good interview, study background information on the man you selected. Then write 10 to 12 questions on topics you would most like to ask him.

1. _____

_____

2. _____

_____

3. _____

_____

4. _____

_____

5. _____

_____

6. _____

_____

7. _____

_____

8. _____

_____

9. _____

_____

10. _____

_____

11. _____

_____

12. _____

_____

Name: _____ Date: _____

Meet Jacques Cartier

Born: 1491 in Saint Malo, France
Died: 1557

In spite of all the unexplored land and bountiful natural resources of the New World, the French and English monarchs had little thought of colonizing the area at first. They believed it would be more profitable to find a water route across North America to China and the riches of the East.

Not much is known of the early life of Jacques Cartier. He grew up in a seaport on the northwestern coast of France. After reading John Cabot's reports of the great schools of fish off the North American coast, fleets of French fisherman began traveling to Newfoundland early in the sixteenth century. Cartier may have joined those fishing expeditions in his youth.

While the Spanish explored South America and the southern United States, France commissioned Jacques Cartier to search for a waterway west to the Pacific Ocean.

While on fishing expeditions, he would have had the opportunity to meet many of the Native Americans, learn some of their language, and explore inland waterways. His experiences may have been what convinced King Francis I of France to allow Cartier to lead an expedition in 1534 to search for a water passage across North America to the Pacific Ocean.

On his first voyage, Cartier crossed the Atlantic Ocean with two ships and 60 men in only 20 days, about half the time the voyage usually took. He landed first on an island near Newfoundland, then sailed north and west, exploring several inland waterways including the Strait of Belle Isle and the Gulf of St. Lawrence.

Landing near the site of Gaspe, Cartier claimed the land for France. Along the way, Cartier and his crew encountered the Micmacs and established trade with them. Since it was late autumn by then, Cartier decided to return to France.

1. The type of ship on which Cartier sailed was called a caravel, similar to Columbus's ships on his voyages to the New World. Use reference sources to write a description of a caravel on another sheet of paper. Add illustrations to your report.

Name: _____   Date: _____

 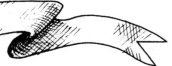

Cartier's Second Voyage

Although he had not found the passage he sought, Cartier told the king of France he had heard of another large river that he hoped would lead to the Pacific Ocean. The king authorized a second voyage in 1535, this time with three ships.

Cartier reached the St. Lawrence River and sailed upriver to the present location of Quebec. There he found Stadacona, a Huron village. The chief, Donnaconna, welcomed the men to *canada,* the Huron word for village.

The expedition continued on to Hochelaga, a fortified village of the Ottawas near where the city of Montreal was later built.

Cartier learned that if he continued, he would soon encounter rapids too dangerous for his ships to navigate. Disappointed, he sailed back to Stadacona where they stayed for the winter. Cartier heard stories from the Hurons about a land in the north called Saguenay, filled with gold and other treasures.

Over the winter, many of Cartier's men developed scurvy. This disease was common to sailors at that time.

Use reference sources to answer these questions.

1. What causes scurvy? _____

   _____

2. What happens to people who have scurvy? _____

   _____

3. How can scurvy be cured? _____

   _____

When he returned to France, Cartier had to admit that he still had not found the promised passageway, that many of his men had died, and that he had brought no riches back for the king.

Cartier wanted to make another expedition immediately to look for Saguenay, but Spain and France were at war. Finally in 1541, the king gave Cartier permission for a third voyage, but not as the leader. This time he would be the assistant to Jean Francois de la Rocque, sieur de Roberval, Viceroy to New France.

4. Use a dictionary. What does *viceroy* mean? _____

   _____

Name: _____   Date: _____

Cartier's Third and Final Voyage

Cartier set sail on his third voyage in 1541 without Roberval.

1. Why do you think Cartier did not wait for Roberval even though the king had commanded him to do so?

    _____

    _____

    Cartier returned to the Huron village of Stadacona where he traded for beaver pelts and other furs. Then he continued his quest for the riches of Saguenay. Along the way, his men collected what they thought were diamonds and gold, but in reality, they were quartz and pyrite.

Use reference sources.

2. Describe quartz: _____

    _____

3. Describe pyrite: _____

    _____

4. What is another name for pyrite?_____

    Cartier returned to Newfoundland in the spring to discover Roberval had finally arrived—a year late. Roberval wanted Cartier to go back to Stadacona while his ships took the furs to France, but Cartier refused and returned to France.

    Unknown to Cartier, one of his crewmen was loyal to Roberval. When they returned to France with the furs, the spy reported to the king that Cartier had discovered gold and diamonds and many more furs that he had kept for himself. Unable to learn which report was true, the king refused to allow Cartier to sail again.

    The king of France and Cartier, himself, considered his voyages a failure because he had not discovered a water route to the Pacific. However, Cartier's explorations were the basis for France's later claim to a large part of Canada.

5. Do you think Cartier was a failure? Why or why not?

    _____

    _____

    _____

Check It Out:
Jacques Cartier, Samuel De Champlain and Explorers of Canada by Tony Coulter
French Explorers of North America by David J. Abodaher

Name: _____   Date: _____

Important Events During Cartier's Lifetime

Use reference sources to create a time line of important historical events during the lifetime of Jacques Cartier.

Year   **Event**

1491   Jacques Cartier born in Saint Malo, France

1492   Columbus sailed on his first voyage to the New World

_____   _____

_____   _____

_____   _____

_____   _____

_____   _____

_____   _____

_____   _____

_____   _____

_____   _____

_____   _____

_____   _____

_____   _____

_____   _____

_____   _____

_____   _____

_____   _____

_____   _____

_____   _____

_____   _____

_____   _____

_____   _____

_____   _____

_____   _____

1557   Jacques Cartier died

Name: _____ Date: _____

Meet Samuel de Champlain

Born: 1567 in Brouage, France
Died: 1635 in Quebec, Canada

Little is known of Samuel de Champlain's early life. From his father, a sea captain, he learned navigation and mapmaking. Champlain served in the army of King Henry IV for several years. His first known voyage was a two-year trip with his uncle around 1599 to Puerto Rico, Mexico, Columbia, the Bermudas, and Panama.

Champlain presented the king with detailed reports and drawings of what he had seen in Central and South America. He was invited by Aymar de Chaste, a fur trader, to join an expedition to Canada in 1603.

Samuel de Champlain wrote to a friend in 1613 that he had acquired an interest "from a very young age in the art of navigation, along with a love of the high seas."

When Champlain arrived, he found the Algonquins and Hurons were in the midst of a war with their enemies, the Iroquois. Champlain and other Frenchmen became allies of the Algonquins and Hurons to protect the French fur trading interests. This alliance later caused many problems for French and English colonists.

From the natives, Champlain learned of a "great water" to the west. Champlain hoped this would be the Pacific Ocean. At last he might be the one who found the elusive water route to India!

Champlain returned to the king of France with his news. The following year he sailed again to Canada as mapmaker and geographer with a group planning to establish a colony. They explored the North American coast as far south as present-day Cape Cod, Massachusetts.

After building a fort at Port Royal, Champlain explored the area and established friendly relations with the Micmacs and other natives before returning to France.

By 1608, Champlain was back in Canada. He chose Stadacona as the most suitable place for a new colony. This eventually became Quebec and was the first permanent city in North America north of Florida to be settled by Europeans.

1. Champlain was a skilled mapmaker and illustrator. Why would these skills be valuable to the king?

_____

_____

Name: _____ Date: _____

Father of New France

      While in France in 1610, Champlain married Helene Boulle, who was only 12 years old at the time. She remained in France for ten years before joining her husband in Canada. Four years later she returned to France, unable to accept the harsh conditions in Canada. After he died, she entered a convent.

1.   How old was Champlain when he got married? _____

      Champlain made several trips between France and Canada. In France, he pleaded with the king for supplies, finances, and people for the colonies. In Canada, he continued to explore lands and waterways to the west and south. He named one of the lakes he discovered for himself, Lake Champlain. He helped establish another colony that later became Montreal. Champlain also became further involved in the war between the Hurons and Algonquins against the Iroquois, and he was wounded several times.

      France and England went to war in 1628. The following year, Quebec was captured by the British. Champlain was taken to England as a prisoner. By then, however, the war had ended. Champlain returned to Canada in 1633 as governor of New France to find Quebec in ruins. He worked to rebuild the city, expand the fur trade, and encourage colonists until his death in 1635.

If you lived in Canada today and wanted to get a message to someone in France, you could make a phone call or send an e-mail. To send news to France, Champlain had to wait for a ship to sail. The trip across the Atlantic usually took four to six weeks, one way. Few ships crossed the Atlantic in winter. It could easily be six months or more from the time he sent a letter until he received a reply.

2.   What types of problems might develop due to this delay in communications? Give specific examples.

     _____

     _____

     _____

3.   Champlain has been called the "Father of New France." Do you think that is appropriate? Why or why not?

     _____

     _____

     _____

Check It Out:
Jacques Cartier, Samuel De Champlain and Explorers of Canada by Tony Coulter
Samuel De Champlain by W. J. Jacobs

Name: _____   Date: _____

Discovering a New World

Imagine being the first person to visit a strange, unknown continent. It's up to you to name the continent and the eight locations marked on the map from the word bank below. Describe what you found at each place, including the people, weather, animals, plants, foods, customs, and so on.

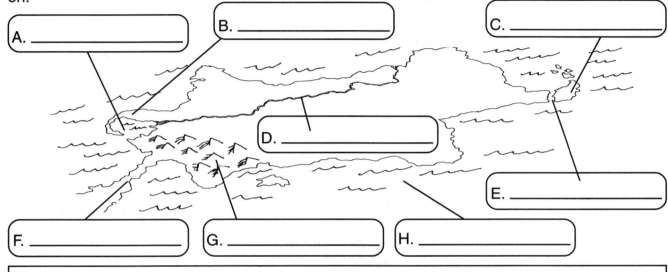

A. _____

B. _____

C. _____

D. _____

E. _____

F. _____

G. _____

H. _____

river	mountain range	delta	bay	isthmus
strait	peninsula	ocean	island	tributary

Name of continent: _____

A. _____
   _____

B. _____
   _____

C. _____
   _____

D. _____
   _____

E. _____
   _____

F. _____
   _____

G. _____
   _____

H. _____
   _____

Name: _____ Date: _____

Meet Henry Hudson

Born: about 1570 in England
Died: date unknown, possibly 1611

Henry Hudson was commissioned by the English Muscovy Company in 1607 to find a shortcut from England to "the islands of spicery." Some geographers theorized that since the days were longer the further north you went, once you got to the Arctic, the sun would be warm enough to melt the ice, and you would eventually reach open water.

As they sailed north, the magnetic needle of the compass was affected, leading crewmen to believe it was caused by an evil spell. They threatened to mutiny.

Hudson sailed to Greenland and north, searching

Little is known of Henry Hudson's early life. He probably had experience sailing because by the time of his first recorded voyage, he was already a captain.

for a passage through the Arctic Ocean to the Far East. Hudson failed in his first two attempts when he ran into ice floes, but he did sail farther north than any other previous explorer—about 577 nautical miles from the North Pole.

1. Use a dictionary. What is an ice floe? _____

_____

On his second voyage for the Muscovy Company in 1608, Hudson sailed through the Arctic waters north of Russia as far as Novaya Zemlya. Again, ice blocked the ship, and he had to return to England.

2. Find Novaya Zemlya on a world map. If it hadn't been for the ice floes, would it have been possible for Hudson to reach India if he had continued in that direction?

_____

3. Would that route be longer or shorter than sailing around the southern tip of Africa to reach India?

_____

4. Use a world map. If it weren't for the ice floes, would it be possible to sail from England, around Greenland, and on to India?

_____

5. Would that route be longer or shorter than sailing around the southern tip of Africa to reach India?

_____

Name: _____ Date: _____

Hudson's Fate Unknown

The Dutch East India Company of the Netherlands, which had a monopoly on trade with the Orient, also wanted to shorten the lengthy and expensive route around the southern tip of Africa. They hired Hudson in 1609, provided a ship, the *Halve Maan (Half Moon),* and a crew of Dutch and English sailors. Again Hudson tried sailing east, north of Norway, but soon turned his ship around and headed for the New World.

Hudson sailed to North America and explored the river later named for him, going as far as present-day Albany, New York, before the river became too shallow to continue. Because Hudson had been sent by a company from the Netherlands, the Dutch later laid claim to land in this area.

When he returned to England, he was arrested for sailing under another nation's flag. The *Half Moon* and its Dutch crew went home. Hudson was commanded to serve only England.

1. Even before Columbus, it was common for captains from one country to sail for a foreign monarch. Why do you think England finally decided not to allow any Englishmen to sail under another country's flag?

   _____

   _____

   _____

   _____

   _____

   _____

The following year, a group of wealthy London merchants sent Hudson on another voyage as captain of the *Discovery,* still in search of a northwest passage. Hudson sailed to Iceland, into the Hudson Strait, and on to Hudson Bay. Trapped by ice in James Bay, the crew was forced to winter there. Over the winter, the crew mutinied and set Hudson, his son, and seven others adrift in a small open boat in 1611. They were never seen again.

2. On another sheet of paper, write a fictional story about the fate of Henry Hudson and his companions who were set adrift in 1611.

Three years later, at the insistence of his wife, Katherine, the Dutch East Indies Company sent a ship to look for Hudson and his men, but no trace of them was ever found. Hudson and his wife had three sons: Richard, John, and Oliver. John was abandoned with his father. Several of Richard's children later migrated to the New World.

Check It Out:
Beyond the Sea of Ice: Voyages of Henry Hudson by Joan Elizabeth Goodman

Name: _____ Date: _____

Meet René Robert Cavelier, Sieur de La Salle

Born: November 22, 1643, in Rouen, France
Died: 1687

The French explorer, Robert La Salle, explored the length of the Mississippi River, claiming the entire area for France.

Historical sources agree that Robert La Salle spent eight or nine years studying with the Jesuits, but they do not agree on whether or not he became a priest. He immigrated to Canada in 1666 and was granted land on the St. Lawrence River, where he became a trader. From 1669 to 1670, he explored the region south of Lakes Ontario and Erie, discovering the Ohio River in 1671.

During his travels, La Salle became familiar with many of the Native American tribes, their languages, and customs. He was appointed commander of Fort Frontenac (Kingston, Ontario), a trading station, and put in charge of the fur trade in that area.

La Salle heard tales of a great river system that he thought might flow across North America. Like others before him, he hoped to find a water passage across the continent. He began his first major explorations in 1669.

In 1677, La Salle received permission to explore and trade to the west. He established forts at the mouth of the St. Joseph River and along the Illinois River.

La Salle and a party of French and Native Americans sailed down the Mississippi to the Gulf of Mexico in 1682. He claimed all land drained by the river for Louis XIV, king of France, and named the region Louisiana.

1. On the map, use red to trace a water route from Fort Frontenac through the Great Lakes to the St. Joseph River.

2. On the map, use blue to trace a water route from Fort St. Joseph to the Gulf of Mexico.

Name: _____ Date: _____

A Disastrous Adventure

When La Salle returned to France in 1683, the king received him as a hero and named him Viceroy of North America. The following year, he sent La Salle with four ships to establish a colony for France at the mouth of the Mississippi River. They sailed around Florida, through the Gulf of Mexico, and landed on the shore of Matagorda Bay, Texas.

1. On the map on the previous page, circle the Gulf of Mexico and Matagorda Bay. Use green to show where the Mississippi meets the Gulf of Mexico.

At first, La Salle believed the bay was the western outlet of the Mississippi River but then realized his mistake. Of his four ships, two sank, one was captured by the Spanish, and the other returned to France, leaving the colonists stranded and without supplies. Many died from disease, rattlesnake bites, and attacks by unfriendly natives.

La Salle and a small group of men set out for Canada in 1687 on foot, leaving behind about 20 settlers who had survived. His men mutinied and killed him near the Trinity River. A few of the survivors eventually made it to Quebec.

The *Belle,* one of La Salle's supply ships that sank in 1686, was discovered in Matagorda Bay in 1995 in only 12 feet of water. Marine archaeologists have recovered the hull of the ship and one skeleton. There were also bronze cannons bearing the crest of Louis XIV; thousands of blue, white, and black glass trade beads; and other artifacts well preserved in the sand and mud.

2. Use reference sources to learn what else was found on La Salle's sunken ship, the *Belle.* List what has been found and what scientists have learned by studying the ship.

_____

_____

_____

_____

_____

_____

_____

_____

Check It Out:
La Salle and the Exploration of the Mississippi by Daniel Marmon
La Salle: A Life of Boundless Adventure by William Jay Jacobs
René-Robert Cavelier Sieur de La Salle by Jim Hardgrove

Name: _____ Date: _____

Let's Review

Matching.

____	1. Robert La Salle	A.	Sailed for the Dutch East India Company in search of a northwest water passage to India
____	2. Henry Hudson		
____	3. *canada*	B.	La Salle's recovered sunken ship
____	4. The *Belle*	C.	Father of New France
____	5. caravel	D.	Area claimed by La Salle for King Louis XIV of France
____	6. Stadacona	E.	Huron village visited by Cartier
____	7. Claimed land along the Mississippi for France	F.	Type of ship Cartier sailed
		G.	Explored Mississippi River to Gulf of Mexico
____	8. Samuel de Champlain	H.	Huron word for "village"
____	9. The *Half Moon*	I.	Robert La Salle
____	10. Louisiana	J.	Henry Hudson's Dutch ship

Use the Venn diagram below to compare any two explorers. Include ways they were alike in the center of the two circles and ways they were different in the two outer parts of the circles.

Name #1: _____   Name #2: _____

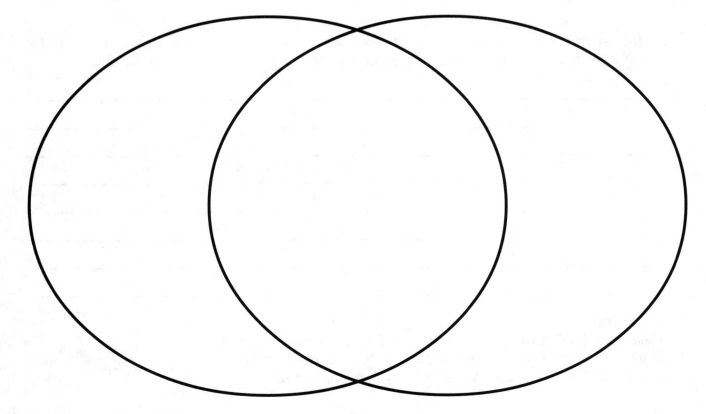

Name: _____ Date: _____

Which Came First?

Use reference sources and the time line on page 2. Circle the number of the event in each group that came first.

A. 1. Christopher Columbus sailed to the New World
   2. Marco Polo traveled to China
   3. John Cabot explored Newfoundland

B. 1. Vasco da Gama discovered a sea route around Africa
   2. Vasco Balboa discovered the Pacific Ocean
   3. Ponce de León searched for the fountain of youth

C. 1. Ferdinand Magellan was born
   2. Christopher Columbus was born
   3. Amerigo Vespucci was born

D. 1. Henry Hudson sailed to North America
   2. Sebastian Cabot sailed to North America
   3. Christopher Columbus died

E. 1. Cortés conquered the Aztecs
   2. Ferdinand Pizarro conquered the Incas
   3. Coronado searched for the Seven Cities of Cíbola

F. 1. Cortés founded Veracruz
   2. Jamestown founded
   3. Colony at St. Augustine founded

G. 1. Champlain founded Quebec
   2. William Shakespeare born
   3. Henry Hudson set adrift by mutineers

H. 1. La Salle tried to establish colony at mouth of Mississippi River
   2. Sebastian Cabot explored Hudson Bay area
   3. Hudson searched for a northwest passage to India

I. 1. Colonists held the Boston Tea Party
   2. William Penn founded Pennsylvania
   3. Pilgrims landed in Plymouth

List three historical events that occurred between 1500 and 1650 not mentioned in this book. Write the events in order and include the dates they occurred.

1. _____

_____

2. _____

_____

3. _____

_____

Name: _____ Date: _____

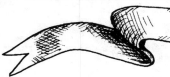

Where Were They From?

Write the last names of these explorers on the lines by the country where they were born.
Review what you learned or use reference sources to help you.

1. Vasco Núñez de Balboa
2. John Cabot
3. Sebastian Cabot
4. Jacques Cartier
5. Samuel de Champlain
6. Christopher Columbus
7. Francisco Coronado
8. Hernan Cortés
9. Hernando de Soto

10. Vasco da Gama
11. Henry Hudson
12. Robert La Salle
13. Juan Ponce de León
14. Ferdinand Magellan
15. Francisco Pizarro
16. Amerigo Vespucci

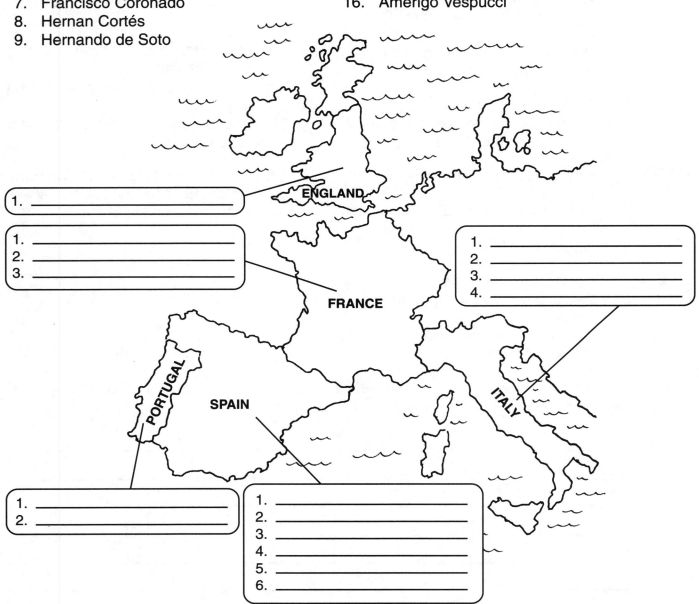

Name: _____ Date: _____

Setting Up a New Colony

The year is 1600. You are planning to start your own settlement in the New World. You will need people who have useful skills for the new colony.

1. List the ten skills you think will be most important.

   _____   _____

   _____   _____

   _____   _____

   _____   _____

2. Number the skills from 1 to 10 in the order you think is most important.

3. List the types of animals that should be included for the new colony.

   _____

   _____

4. List the types of plants or seeds you plan to take.

   _____

   _____

   _____

5. List tools people will need and why they will need them. For example: a hammer to build homes.

   _____

   _____

   _____

   _____

6. List other items and why they would be needed to set up a new colony.

   _____

   _____

   _____

   _____

Name: _____ Date: _____

Searching for the Explorers

Match the first and last names of these famous explorers.

_____	1. Amerigo	A.	Balboa
_____	2. Christopher	B.	Cabot
_____	3. Francisco	C.	Cartier
_____	4. Giovanni	D.	Champlain
_____	5. Henry	E.	Columbus
_____	6. Hernan	F.	Coronado
_____	7. Jacques	G.	Cortés
_____	8. Ferdinand	H.	de León
_____	9. John	I.	Erickson
_____	10. Leif	J.	Hudson
_____	11. Ponce	K.	La Salle
_____	12. Robert	L.	Magellan
_____	13. Samuel	M.	Verrazzano
_____	14. Vasco	N.	Vespucci

Look up, down, backwards, forwards, and diagonally to find the first and last names (separately) of the explorers in the puzzle.

```
Y J F I L K A Y G R E I T R A C W J N F
N P L L S O Q M Q K R S A M U E L N Y Y
A W L X B E I H K F R A N C I S C O Y D
L J E L T Q T O C S A V P F D E E Z M E
L O A Y U S T R B R U H N K S A R J S Y
E B S U B M U L O C H R I S T O P H E R
G W K D B P P I K C V E R R A Z Z A N O
A C R D E W H X D U F Z D T N S W D B L
M V N J F L D E P T Q H D H I T Q Q I E
K B O O E D E O O P V L N O A R M F E X
U H T D R O N O N W A E H S L E U P A E
N U O A D C C C N M T I F X P B V L A D
Q T B N E E X B E S S F H R M O I I S N
N O A O X W R R W F E C E W A R C J E A
W H C R V M I I S M L X R B H G C U U N
W U K O P G B P C L L F N Y C S U G Q I
R D J C O J E D E K A O A K R Q P T C D
D S Z U G I Y J H V S M N X I N S P A R
F O P B R B S B H C A O F R V H E W J E
C N I N N A V O I G L W N E C R V H I F
```

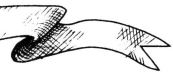

Name: _____ Date: _____

Setting Up a Space Colony

Someday people may venture into space and establish a colony on a space station or even on another planet. Whether you were planning to establish a new colony on Earth in 1600 or starting a new colony in space, many of the needs people have would remain the same: food, water, shelter, and clothing. They would need certain tools and medicines.

1. How would setting up a space colony be similar to starting an Earth colony in the 1600s?

_____

_____

_____

_____

_____

_____

2. How would setting up a space colony be different from starting an Earth colony in the 1600s?

_____

_____

_____

_____

_____

_____

3. Which do you think would be more difficult? Explain your answer.

_____

_____

_____

_____

_____

_____

Learn About Other Explorers

Learn more about another great explorer. Write a report on one of the people listed below. Include when and where they were born, where they explored, and why they are famous. Use maps and illustrations to make your report more interesting.

Marco Polo
Henry the Navigator
Bartholomew Diaz
Pedro Alvares Cabral
Francisco de Orellana
Sir Martin Frobisher
Sir Frances Drake
Bartholomew Gosnold
Robert Edwin Peary
William Baffin
Abel Janszoon Tasman
Jacques Marquette
Louis Jolliet
Vitus Bering
Sir Alexander Mackenzie
George Vancouver
Meriwether Lewis

Robert Edwin Peary

William Clark
Zebulon Montgomery Pike
John Charles Frémont
David Livingstone
Nikolai Przhevalski
Sir Henry Stanley
Nils Nordenskjold
Fridtjof Nansen
Roald Amundsen
Sir Douglas Mawson
Sir Ernest Henry Shackleton
James Cook
Roy Chapman Andrews
Robert Falcon Scott
Donald Baxter MacMillan
Umberto Nobile
Richard Evelyn Byrd
Sir Edmund Hillary

James Cook

60

Answer Key

Who Came First? (page 3)
1. One who travels in an unknown or little-known region
2. People who are offspring, however remote, of a certain ancestor, family, or group
3. To move from one place to another; to move from one region to another with the change in seasons
4. A tribe or people having no permanent home, but moving about constantly in search of food, pasture, etc.

Sailing to The Americas (page 4)
1. Norway, Sweden, and Denmark are considered Scandinavian countries; also sometimes Iceland and the Faeroe Islands.

The Lands of the Vikings (page 7)
1. Iceland
2. Greenland
3. Norway
4. Baffin Island
5. Labrador
6. Teacher check

Meet Christopher Columbus (page 8)
1. King Ferdinand and Queen Isabella of Spain
2. 1492, 1493, 1498, and 1502
3. Answers will vary. There are over 60 places in the United States named for Columbus, including the District of Columbia; Columbia, South Carolina; and Columbus, Ohio.

The Four Voyages of Columbus (page 9)
1-3. Teacher check map.
4. The fourth voyage appears to be the longest.

Fact or Fiction? (page 10)
1. Fact
2. Fact
3. Fiction
4. Fact
5. Fact
6. Fact
7. Fiction
8. Fact

Trade With the Far East (page 11)
1. Africa
2. To find a water route to India
3. Many of the crew died from scurvy. They encountered many fierce storms and had several battles along the east coast of Africa with Muslim traders who did not want the Portuguese to interfere with their trade.
4. The voyage took over two years. They left Lisbon in July, 1497, and returned in September, 1499
5. One could reach India by sailing east around Africa.

Meet Vasco Núñez de Balboa (page 12)
1. Venezuela
2. He ran a plantation.
3. A friend smuggled him off the island in a barrel to escape his creditors.
4. None of those crops grew in Europe.

Sighting the Pacific Ocean (page 13)
2a. The conducting of relations between nations
   b. Violation of the allegiance owed to one's sovereign or state; betrayal of one's country
   c. A narrow strip of land having water at each side and connecting two larger bodies of land

Meet Amerigo Vespucci (page 16)
1. The art and work of making maps or charts
2. The science of the universe, in which the stars, planets, etc., are studied
3. This knowledge would help an explorer calculate time and distance, navigate by using the sun and stars, and record where he had been
4. One who plots the course or steers a ship or aircraft
5. 45 years old

Meet John Cabot (page 18)
1. 54 days

A Charter From the King (page 19)
2. 20 percent
3. No one could visit the lands the Cabots had discovered without their permission.

Meet Sebastian Cabot (page 21)
1. No
2. Revolt against authority, especially rebellion of soldiers or sailors against their officers

Magellan Circumnavigates the Earth (page 23)
1. To sail or fly completely around the earth
2. He believed he could find a passage to India through or around South America.
3. Magellan was killed in a battle on Cebu Island.
4. South America, Asia, Africa, Europe
5. The earth is round.

Let's Review (page 24)
1. C
2. H
3. F
4. E
5. J
6. A
7. B
8. M
9. G
10. D
11. N
12. L
13. I
14. K

Answer Key

Conquest of the Aztecs (page 31)

2. An act or state of armed resistance to one's government; a defiance of any authority or control
3. To pronounce free from guilt or blame

More Treachery (page 35)

1. A leader whose actions and ideas are controlled by another person

Fact or Fiction?

1. Fact
2. Fact
3. Fact
4. Fact

What Did Coronado Really Discover? (page 38)

A. California
B. Arizona
C. New Mexico
D. Texas
E. Kansas
F. Arkansas
G. Oklahoma

Let's Review (page 41)

1. I
2. E
3. L
4. J
5. F
6. K
7. B
8. G
9. C
10. H
11. O
12. N
13. A
14. D
15. M

Cartier's Second Voyage (page 44)

1. A lack of ascorbic acid (Vitamin C) in the body
2. They become weak and develop anemia, spongy gums, and bleeding from the mucous membranes.
3. Give the person foods high in Vitamin C.
4. A person ruling a country, province, or colony as the deputy of a sovereign

Cartier's Third and Final Voyage (page 45)

2. It is a crystalline mineral that may be clear or colored and can be used as a semiprecious stone.
3. It is a shiny, yellow mineral often embedded in rock.
4. Fool's gold

Father of New France (page 48)

1. 43 years old

Discovering a New World (page 49)

A. bay
B. peninsula
C. island
D. river
E. strait
F. isthmus
G. mountain range
H. ocean

Meet Henry Hudson (page 50)

1. A single piece, large or small, of floating sea ice
2. Yes
3. Longer
4. Yes
5. Longer

Meet René Robert Cavelier, Sieur de La Salle (page 52)

1.–2. Teacher check map.

A Disastrous Adventure (page 53)

1. Teacher check map on page 52.

Let's Review (page 54)

1. G
2. A
3. H
4. B
5. F
6. E
7. I
8. C
9. J
10. D

Which Came first? (page 55)

A. 2
B. 1
C. 2
D. 3
E. 1
F. 1
G. 3
H. 2
I. 3

Where Were They From? (page 56)

1. Vasco Núñez de Balboa — Spain
2. John Cabot — Italy
3. Sebastian Cabot — Italy
4. Jacques Cartier — France
5. Samuel de Champlain — France
6. Christopher Columbus — Italy
7. Francisco Coronado — Spain
8. Hernan Cortés — Spain
9. Hernando de Soto — Spain
10. Vasco da Gama — Portugal
11. Henry Hudson — England
12. Robert La Salle — France
13. Juan Ponce de León — Spain
14. Ferdinand Magellan — Portugal
15. Francisco Pizarro — Spain
16. Amerigo Vespucci — Italy

Searching for the Explorers (page 58)

1. N
2. E
3. F
4. M
5. J
6. G
7. C
8. L
9. B
10. I
11. H
12. K
13. D
14. A

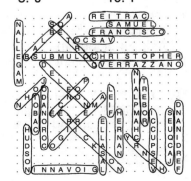